Poetry of life

Anagha Donekal

BookLeaf Publishing

Presentation by *BookLeaf Publishing*

Web: www.bookleafpub.com

E-mail: info@bookleafpub.com

ISBN: 9789358737202

First edition 2023

Mom , Dad and my Elder sister Yamini

Preface

Poetry has been a passion of mine for many years. I started writing poems when I was a child. Literature has been a part of my life, hearing and reading Ramayana, Mahabharata and the Puranas. I grew up knowing about the importance of sacrifice, the need for love in one's life and to always be surrounded by love and affection. Being the younger sibling, I grew up as a very pampered child. But my poetry always had a philosophical edge which you will notice in the following pages. But I won't give you any spoilers yet. Enjoy yourselves is all I have to say.

Acknowledgement

I would like to thank my elder sister Yamini with brother-in-law Sushanth, my mom Shamala and dad Sreepathi who have been there for me at every step of my journey. This is my first book. Hope everyone who reads likes it.

Ocean of Time

Time and tide wait for none
This is a proverb all should learn
As time once lost never returns

Make the best use of time that you can
As past is past and future is future
But present is what it is now
So make the best use of now as now will never
again come

Life on earth is terribly short
To waste on things that are hopelessly useless
Stop wasting your time oh children
Instead find your goal in life
For time and tide wait for none
Is a terrific proverb to learn.

Feast in the Playground

As I was driving I heard voices
Joyous voices of kids , kids playing
In the park on swings and slides
I looked in wonder at the sight
For it was indeed a feast to the eyes

Children laughing and running around
Oh, how long it has been since I ran
I got out and walked towards the park
Drinking in the sight before me

Like a child I ran to the slide
And climbing up slid down joyfully
People stared but did I care
It was the happiest moment in my memory

Since then I do the thing I like
Playing with children and elders alike
Oh why do I care if people stare
For happiness is all I care

The Player of Fate

The Player of fate, who could it be
The one who knows everything
The one who can do anything
Play any game with his cleverness

Who could it be ? Is that your question ?
It's the almighty God who is called differently
By various religions like Jesus for Christians
Vishnu for Hindus and Allah for Muslims

Does he have a form? someone asked
Well that's an answer all of us want
For no one has seen him for whom he is

How do you see him? someone asked
Well that's a question I have an answer for
Yoga, meditation and chanting of God's name
Will give you what you want

In this Kali Yuga chant his name
For a couple of times and then
The player of fate will give you what you want

A Cloudy Day

The sun was shining brightly in the sky
But dark clouds were approaching quickly
Children were playing in the playground
But the clouds sealed the playground like a
coffin .

All the children cried out , oh let it rain
So that we can all get wet
The wind blew vigorously shaking the trees
All the children stopped and looked towards the
sky

As raindrops fell from the sky
Soon it was raining heavily
All children tried to get as wet as possible
But the teachers called them angrily

All children went to the class as slowly as
They possibly could, dripping wet on the stony
floor
All crowded to look outside the window
But alas the heavy rain had stopped suddenly

Recipe for Success

Like a spoon full of sugar
A glass full of milk
A little amount of coffee
Makes a heartwarming drink.

So too a spoonful of desire
A glass full of concentration
A cup full of hard work and focus
Will yield the sweet fruit called success

People who think but never act are daydreamers
Those people can never achieve their goal
But people who strive and sweat for it
Have all their dreams come true

People who try, achieve success, so
Why can't other people achieve it ?
People have their own potent
Bring out that inborn potent in you
And success is a step away if hard work is there.

The Change

From the top of the tower, I stared
Into the distance far away
The orange blaze of the setting sun ,
Was indeed a beautiful sight to see .

In that place I made a plan
To change my life for the better
To seek out chances, to achieve success
To make my life a better one

First my life , than the society
Wiping out all its bad things
In the orange blaze of the setting sun
I made a plan for change .

In the morning

Standing outside the house I stared
At the beautiful feast for the eyes
On the horizon the sun rose
In the beautiful blue sky

Birds chirped; leaves rustled
To meet another beautiful day
People aged and young alike awoke
To meet and greet another great day

On this day the sunlight shone
In through doors, windows and cracks and
creaks
As they were dusted noisily
Thus people all around got ready to start
Another joy filled day

The Ocean

On the shore of the ocean, I sat
Looking at the beautiful blue ocean
Seagulls flew above, sandy soil lay below
And the smell of the ocean was in the air

As I watched children building sand dunes
I thought why build empty castles in our mind
Filling it with empty promises and failures
Build your mind with steel, not sandy soil

Having a strong mind helps build a strong will
With willpower one can achieve anything ,
From the task of going next door
To travelling around the world in eighty days .

Dream but making all your dreams true
Is the achievement you should get
Put all those empty promises and failures away
Start a new chapter in life, and success is yours
if
Your will is strong steel and not sandy soil .

My Teacher

Mother is said to be the first teacher
The father the second and then the school
But last but not the least , life is
Said to be the best teacher of all .

Like a bud blooms into a beautiful flower
So too a teacher helps one to grow into
An amazing individual , with great values ,
Virtues and the discipline , which must be
installed

Life has many tests but how you
Solve them makes you a great individual
A pure heart , a bright intellect ,
Makes you the individual you want to be .

Life

Life is like glass, handle it carefully
For if something goes wrong things may end
badly
There is one very important thing in life
Everyone knows what that is - Happiness
When happiness prevails all is there

There are two paths given by God
The good path and the bad one,
But what is chosen is in one's own hands
What happens in the future is in our hands
So, take the opportunity and choose wisely

There are rocky and smooth paths in life
Everything that happens has a purpose behind
Soon ending with the sweet honey of happiness
So, choose wisely for you have one try only .

Baby

Sweet thing so pretty you are
With toothless little mouth and pretty eyes
Your small feet kicking and hands in fists
Oh, such a delicate being you are

God sent you to earth from heaven
To bring joy to everyone present
Seeing your smile and cry
Whichever is more delightful
A baby's first cry or smile

Little Boy

Naughty boy oh how many times
Will you break the window

Haven't I told you not to play
But Mama, you said yourself that
All work and no play makes Jack a dullboy
Well my son for making you play
My punishment is a broken window

Now go and do your work like a good little boy
For Mama will spank you if you do otherwise
Ran inside when I heard a loud noise
Oh what have you done said I with tears in my
eyes

Nothing ma the vase fell by itself said my son
Little devil thinking I took a cane to spank him
But off he went out through the broken window
pane

Sorry

As far as I can look back today
Into the past dark and grey
I always saw you throughout
Holding my hand and guiding me all the way .

I never had a chance to say thank you for all you
did
Being blind to the love and support given by you
So sorry mum and sorry dad for making you cry
For all the mistakes and mishaps committed
As little girls do mistakes sometimes .

For now and ever I promise to listen to you
Always as you are so good
This is a small gift to you with a promise of
change
Please forgive me and let's start a new chapter in
life
For I know there's a whole lifetime ahead
To make you laugh again .

Gone

For years and years, you've been gone
Come back, oh please come back
Can't you see how much I've missed you tonight

I can never live without you never have I or ever
can I
Being with you in my dreams is never enough
For I yearn to hear your voice telling me
Everything is going to be alright
When I do something which isn't right

So lonely so left out is my feeling without you
Always wishing to see you once more in my life
Again, hearing stories of princes and princesses
While lying on a bed with my head on your lap
Back to normal as if you never left me and went
away.

Silence

Silence, it is almost deafening tonight
As I look at the future so dark and lonely

Come out and save me tonight
For I don't think if I can survive it anymore
But with you by my side
You know I can face the whole wide world

So please come back to me ,
You won't lack love anymore in your life
For I'll love you forever and ever
You won't even know how the days have
become years

With me by your side and you by mine
We can face the world tonight

New year

The bells of the church are ringing
A distant echo in the forest

It's time, it's time says someone there
Everyone gathers around at once
To count ten , nine, eight, seven
Till the number zero
Hurray everyone gathered says
Kissing each other and congratulating them
To welcome the beginning of a new year

Little One

Come with me, to the other place
A place you would have only imagined
One you would have dreamed of

There is so much to see out there
That you have only heard about
While sleeping in your place with your tiny eyes
closed up

To bring joy to this world
Come out little one out of your coconned resting
place
Into this big wide world
To bring joy in this place and wherever you go

The Valley

Walking in the pale moonlight I
In a valley where even the dead made no sound
Surrounded by trees all around
With only a ray of light to guide myself

When all of a sudden an ear - piercing voice
Echoes through the night
So forlorn that even the animals cowered in fear

Searching for the voice I go but alas with little
success
Till I reach the valley's edge
And from then till now
The voice from the valley echoes in my dreams
Like a ghost whispering continually

My World

When you were born little one
It was like the whole world lit up at once
For the first time in my life
I knew joy, I knew happiness in my life
For I had never seen someone so fragile

There were no words which I could think
To describe you - beautiful, delicate, the most
sweet thing
As you opened your little eyes
To look at me with those big innocent eyes
My little bundle of joy

Memories at Night

I sat by the window side
Leaning my body against the glass
Watching the rain patter against the glass
Reminding me of all those painful memories
Silence and horror vibrated in my heart
Thinking back to the oh so painful days

Shaking as I sobbed both out of sorrow and fear
Fearing the cold dark unknown in the front
Searching but finding not but a single light
Praying that the awful history of bygone days
Repeats itself no more

The Tunnel

A dark passage winding down
Walking on but couldn't find
What I was looking for
Just a ray of light coming through
To guide me as I walked in
Searching for that someone for so long

The passage never seems to end
Leading me once more there
In the same old stony cold cave
With twists and turns as I walk on
Within my reach but always why so far

The Candle

A lone candle flickering in the dark
In the pale glow of the moonlight
A happy thought passes my mind
Like a warm afternoon breeze

Alone and freezing in the warm afternoon
A candle flickers as it does
Slowly but surely raising in the afternoon
Till the flame melts the ice
Around and surrounds in a warm afterglow
Casting all in a warm afternoon breeze

The Other Side

Riding high never knowing
What the bottom line looked like
And felt like in its harshness
Makeup wise superior and oh so bright I was

Now I know the superior brightness
Is full in its fondness
Having found the light
In a cave of darkness

Thank You

Thank you, a word so small
Yet means so much
Not said enough on a weekday
Or be it the weekend

So much done in the course
Day in and day out everyday
So good and gentle
To teach and to grasp too

A message so deep in its depth
Meaning, too much a thought
Thank you again and once again
Thank you, a word so small but meaning so big
To you and the rest

Sweet Story

A burden am I, a difficult one
To be sure of, safe and protected
Never let out, all the same
From the first till the now

Freedom, a silver thread of
Freewill to go along with it
Crowded around the pathway
Not a single thing to express
By me, myself and I
In this beautiful story of life

Tabula Rasa

Footsteps, baby ones at a time
From an embryo to a human one
Learning anew from the first letter
Alphabet abcd, to a twinkle in the sky

A blank slate am I to be written on
Freshly, for a whole new start
With a mind obedient to the will
To control, so as to be happy
For the coming day, which
Could who would say be
A start to a bright joy filled day.

A Companion

A light in the dark
Walking along alone, but just
Not so lonely, for with me
You are, always beside me

Wherever I go, be it even
To the opposite ends of the earth
Forever you will be caring
With a heart full of love

Sharing a story, looking around
A sweet story of a life with you
God you are all I want
Be it in my hardships and cures

A Flower

Sands of time, all in one
Away ticked the time, fast
But not in the least to say
Tick tock and again came a
Tick tock, tick tock tick

Once a baby, now an adult
All grown up swiftly and smart
Like the flower bud blooming
To a beautiful and a colorful
A height to rise into, a great
Wonderful and a magnificent flower

A Gift

A gift, an offering to give
Like a hug is free to go
So too is love up for offer
The more it is shared, the
Higher is the dividend pair

A bright day full of sunshine
Matters not if you keep or give
On and on the day goes on
Till the end of the day
For time oh my precious
Is but for a limited period.

The Face

A question be asked of the girl
Now in the far above, does
She take the fellow who is
Simply and full of love

A person who, gentle and kind
Sweet but a little bit, shy
As a newborn cuddle kitten
Who with big eyes and an adorable smile
Pulls a smart face in case
For the individual and the worldly place

The Sunlight

A star, a bright star to follow
Showing a shine, a brilliant shine
To follow through a goal to keep
The ground we walk on
To make a dream a reality

In the reel world and the
Real world where the sun
Shining a bright ray in the sky
For now, bring a hope light
In the bright skylight.

The Other Side of Life

Life is a pot of milk
Sometimes overflows, a lot to say
A spoon of sugar gives it happiness
But a little salt makes it dangerous

Choose wisely, but choose safely
Life is full of joys and sorrows too
A journey to go on, so as to learn
For if you flip a coin any side can come

Both sides makes life worth living
To make a person strong and to shine
Life is worthy of living if
There are opportunities to drown and climb

The Javan

A little food to eat, shelter is
But a dream to see
Love and affection, a far sighted
Fantasy and a fiction in a book to read

But love for the motherland a reality
First the land of mine, a gift
To safeguard and protect always
Keeping the people first and then
A thought about myself later comes
For security of country , in any condition
A love to fulfill in a keep.

A Salute

My love, my affection to the bravehearts
Who since a child bear a love
For the motherland which is only one
Safeguard and look after the land
Day and night so, when sleeping we can breathe
easily

A thank you to the one who lays
On the border a sacrifice to raise
So we the people can live a life
Worthy and with dignity, whenever it may be

Color of Life

Black or white, a life
Filled with the truth a person
Can see or unsee in a moment's pause
To bring change is destiny's will

Could fill with the colors
A rainbow has, in a ray of light
Choose, but choice be in the right
For only black and white is a life
Filled with dullness indeed, but color
Makes one's life worthy of

Color in the make it
World living , so much so
A multicolour in the life
Brings a power in living seat

A Chance

Open in expression and experience
A person understands, for
Being open helps to make a life
Full of love, a sense to opine
To make or break an individual

Respond and make it worth
To listen, so to achieve by
Once a wrong then learnt
A repeat not to a humble start

The Truth

Truth, a word so small, but
A meaning, whose depth immeasurable
An intangible thing it is
Can't be seen, touched nor smelled

It can however be observed, be it
A verbal or a non verbal saying
In the actions of a person
Or a spoken word, which is of immense power

A Mission

A mission, with a vision ahead
Goal in hand, time alot
Work on it, with a singular mind
For the effort put in
Success comes with a lot of
Hardwork and hardships on it in

With the work done, nothing
In the individual's life is undone
Impossible is a word unknown
For the person on a mission

A Look

A look, say give me
To make my life worth living
Seeing and believing is my role
Begot from the passion
Which is a must to get

Riding high, never understood
The people who are under me
Save in a moment of sympathy
The role of empathy in
An individual's life is a need
Never to go with I , me, myself
But what is the need of the other
Comes first in life , then a thought
Be given to oneself, to live life

The Guide

Love, gives a positive outlook
To see the world as a happy place
Filled fully with good people
To never give up on a mission in life

With a vision at hand
Trust the person who is
There for you the whole day
And everyday, in a year
Through the lifespan, of the person
Always through, seeing and guiding
To make the individual a better one

The Start

A beautiful sunrise just beyond
To look and enjoy all around
A sunrise and a sunset
In the morning and night time too

When bad happens good is always
Right round the corner of the sideway
To bring a new light into the life
Of an individual to make it
Bright and whole again for a new start

The Unique Self

An ancient as the self is
In the beautiful ocean of life
An approach that is needed, unique
Like each new born baby

Looking at the big picture and
Understanding the secret to make
Or break the individual in the seat
Life is a big balancing act, handle it
Carefully, for each person a new
Method is required to bring about a change
By making the other happy, pleasure is yours too

No Expectations

To bring happiness in the life
Of each person that we meet
Small acts of kindness without expectations
Giving everything of myself to the other

First comes the other in life
Then alone comes a thought to the self
Making or breaking the individual self
A happy unique person
Concentration on the needs of the
Other person comes first then a say to the self

An Emotional Phase

Excitement is an emotional phase
That makes a thing happen
Be it during the light of day
Or the darkness of a night

A tense moment, a worry be
Makes the individual fully
Be it in the college or the home
It happens if the person is a worry bee

Oh my sweet don't be scared
For everything in the memory will be
Easy to remember if you want it to be
Just have faith in yourself and the rest around
To help and make you if a want be
A person to be remembered, for everything
Which is positively a cure in life

A Living to Make

A living to make in this life and the next
A beauty it could turn, just love
And the rest, a soul gentle and beautiful

A happy life to a bad one in this life and the next
An era it could be, a century or two
Making the life of mine and the rest
A peaceful, fruitful but a joyous life

To my family first, a society next
But last but not the least my own self
To a good life it is a nice but a happy
A happy and a problemless
Beautiful life, to make the life of mine
And the rest, humans and animals rest
A happy fulfilling joyous life

Little bit of Love

A worm in a sea full of rice
A sweet in a sea full of spices
What can you do to make it good

Magic could, but not solve the issue
A bit of love, a sweet word
Make the heart a soulmate in this
And a great probability in the next

Just a little cleanmaker in a sea
Full of salt makes a glass full to drink
A maker, a beautiful and clean
In the mind, the heart and the soul

The Fight

A row to live with, for
The mother and child until the fight
Is neither started nor finished
To who should the problem be taken to
For making the individual single again

The person is here for now
Roaming around all the way
To set the goal to seek an enchanting
A desirable life, a happy finite life

A Safe Journey

A work done, a good job indeed
Yes or no is the answer to be
Had, in the eyes of the beholder
What is said is special and new
Each has a different, or similar
Thought process, which is unique so far

An opinion, once given can't be
Revoked or changed for one, who
Wants a different dialogue to themself
To make their life easy and save

One who with hardships strives,
Ahead to go forward in a flow
Will move smoothly to go on
A journey of infinite joy

Freedom

49

The smell of freedom is in the air
To laugh and smile of you so get a chance
Making the people in and around
To lead fulfilled and happy life

Given an opportunity to give to all
Love and affection is a must to give
To everyone in the surrounding
For to give is what I live for
In this life and the next

Infinity

Not understanding and not wanting in life
The infinite goal which is left to be found
Searching everywhere inside and outside too
To be or not to be , that is the question
Answered with a yes or no in life

My desired solution will in the end be
By the individual, set and found definitely
To make the person rise and roam free
In internal and external life to be

A Positive Thought

A smile leads to a happy feeling
Which in turn brings a positive thought
Confidence, a much needed emotion
Can never be bought, but only be felt
To do a good thing or work in life

Searching but never find , in the outside world
Some forget to look inside
For inside is the much searched for light
Improving the self is a major thing
To reach a joy filled mind

Class

Accounting and counting the time
To see when the change will be
Into a bright and happy time
For the whole is more than the parts

A person am I, a good one
Look but only assess the inside
For from within am I brilliant and bright
My class is such to judge on a side

Judge but don't judge a book by its cover
For without knowing you can miss
A lot which is within, but
Has never been seen out by the person themself

Red as Blood

A rise given to a valentine
Symbol of the love they share
Red and beautiful, ever green
Like the lead that holds its thread

The solid soldier in a war ahead
Loses not a single but a dozen
To be pretty sure, to save
A billion lives rescued and saved
There will be a loss no more

Future Me

Running but never reaching
The one who has been beyond my reach
For so long, just there but never
To touch my hand, for
In the bright glow of sunset
You will be truly mine alone

To bring the first bunch of happiness
For I, and myself at last
Never alone but now forever
Seeing in the end which is to be
A bright and novel future ahead

Innocence

Innocent as a white rose
A beauty who has no rival to match
The one about whom when talked about
Gives an internal joy which cannot be
Expressed in a word of two now or ever

The one the post speaks of is a newborn
A baby whose red blush is as sweet
As the laughter which is beyond compare
The smile of a baby is another word
For the happiness which is most awaited

Conflicting Thoughts

A conflict in the mind
There is, on an occasion
When a single thought which is
By waiting to be analyzed
By the person in whose mind it arose

Be it a positive or a negative thought
The mind of the individual will be
Filled with, making the person think I
Mentally and physically strong or weak
Depending solely on the multi thought
Which will in the end make the one a busy bee

Trying for Success

Try and get till you succeed
Is not just a quote to say
For to put in practical use the words
In the game of life which is real
Is the true goal to achieve

An obstacle always comes in life
To bring the individual failure so to say
How to try to climb up to gain
A sweet success in the life is a question
Which is but a big secret waiting to be answered
To learn from it and rise up to great heights

Habits make a Man

A habit is something when done
Over and over in a
Repeated manner gives a perfection in work
Which is hard to get when an individual
Doing a particular task once expects
Expertise got by a decade of experience

Habit is something when done in a
Correct manner brings out satisfaction
A pleasure which cannot be got in
Doing a job for the first time
Time when used judiciously with concentration
The result comes quickly to bring
A happiness which can be enjoyed completely

The Teacher

Love a second nature to the one
A God who comes in the physical form
To bring change in the whole than just one part
So as to make in the person at present
An improvement which in the past
Was heard of but alas failed to be implemented

Everyday to hear and report a different thought
The coming of a new thing in the child of mine
Can be done by only a single individual
The teacher who is part of life
An equivalent to the mother
Who works hard to bring a change
The person whose service is taken in whole
But the returns for the same never given even a
quarter

The Pathway

To be or not to be
To do or not to do a particular practical thing
Is a neat question for which the answer to be
Found in the time left is the purpose
The individual strives towards

If a thing is to be done
How then is it to be done
The question of who, what, when, where
Are all that have to be answered
Before the end goal which, to be reached
The pathway simply, by the individual
Be reached beyond any barrier it be

A Successful Day

A bright sunshine in the morning
To wake with a smile for a new day
With a readiness for anything and everything
Outside in the big wide world

Doing all with a practical goal in mind
For having a unique single one for
Everyday, the day which is to take
Of the years to come in the
Individual of the day for the future
So be it an easy or a difficult next day

The Tenses

A part of one, yet not
Is it a question to think of
But many times done makes it lost
For in the past what it was
In the present make it not

A mistake once made, a learning
For a whole lifetime's sake
To remember, to make no more
The same mistake, like a rehearsal repeatedly
Over and over again, to ruin life ahead

The Change Made About

Once a full mood, now a brightness
Brought about solely by work
A hard life itself gave, a chance
To take,and bring a change
Waiting for a means to make the change

A channel required for her
To change so as to bring a new
Situation and a scene in life
To make herself and those around
Laugh and sing a happy song

The Journey of Life

Amidst the chaos in the room
Moving about a difficulty
But to move about a task given
Without which no more a life

Less that is given making more
The work involved a happiness
A joy which is in doing
Makes the individual satisfied

In the coming future, if in
The current present a thought
Be given, to make the coming time
A happy and safe journey

A Happy Life

A good life it is in the known
Completely focused on the present
With a thought not given to the past
Nor the future, for who knows
What it may hold for a single soul

Living life in the present brings
A joy, filled with satisfaction
For a life lived for every moment
Not I knowing what the next may bring
Is a life worth living for

Perfection

Perfection, a simple word
With a meaning whose depth unknown
A thing which is strived for, right from
One in a million to a billion people's lot

Some strive and achieve the impossible
But the question asked by each and everyone is
What do they have that I as an individual lack?

A respect the self and the equality
Given to each other, everyday so as to
Fulfill an objective on all the days
With an intent to achieve the end goal
Be a thought given to it for
Today or a future, tomorrow date

Truth will Out

A lioness amidst a crowd
Acting as soft as a baby lamb a ramp
Not knowing its true birth would
Be that of a queen of the lot

Roaming around seeking protection
Scared of even a small fist of air
Bringing out the truth is a task in itself
For better to be late than never
To be a leader and not a follower for life

A fresh Start

The truth never once said
Choice made for independent am I
Everybody is the same as the day before
A new start know not when

Smiling with a simple on the sides
A false reflection in the mirror to see
The mind in control by the soul inside
To bring about in life, a fresh
Beginning, a chapter in the story
Which is not so stagnant as the last

A State of Mind

What to do and what not to
A question in the mind all times
Every time a confusion, a state of chaos
When a multitude of choices appear

Making many into a single aim
Is but not a game, for in life
Diverse roads may come
Some good, some appear to be good
A specific choice done correctly
Is the only option for a good future to see

Nature a Gift

A feast for the eyes you are
Long time no see, here giving
The effect of calmness like a balm
Healing the wounds of the past

Although a physical body you have
What is given is a mental wellness
A happiness that no other can give
No matter how hard one tries

The sweetness of nature that is present
In the now can never be replicated again
A service to be given is by saving
For what is present can never be same in
The future which brings an unknown next

Growing Up

To grow, firm be the root
Deep in the ground and the surrounding
Day by day nourishment given
Slowly but surely a beauty it be

A feast to the eyes of
The individual who gazes
Bringing a smile of happiness
To a person in sadness or anger
Changing the situation into
Not filled one, for long time to see

An Emotional Change

Growing up always there for me
Both as a child and a friend for me
A sudden but an expected event
What more can it be

Living now a change in me
A missing piece which it be
Seeing everyday but is
An emotionally difficult time marked
In the life of the individual
Speaking with tears flowing clearly

Lock and Key

Locked in a golden cage
Want to move out, but
Same time want to be inside
Learning a varied type
From anything to everything

The world around in its reality
He there, a source lacking not
Having something in it
To learn and to know
Expect for a way out to reach
A free world out there that be

A Child's Smile

An innocent smile which
Is there on the face of a child
Happiness and a feeling it brings
In deep an inner peace know not
Whose root cause unknown in it all

A child's smile is as fresh
As the joy that is felt
When playing with it whose looks brought
Laughter, for behind the face lies a good
To see no matter who sees
May it be a male or a female

Lessons to Learn

Learning lessons in a failed attempt
For failure is said to be
A step in the direction of change
To a new chapter of success

Success brings a motivation
For failure is not lasting
Not will it not change
For life is ever changing
With it bringing a continuous
Flow of constant changes

If a person has but only a wish
The wish to fulfill a targeted goal
A mission which who might know
Will help the individual
A calmness and inner beauty to show
Life not as it is, but as it should be
In the eyes of the beholder to see

Lockdown Diaries

In a house, all day everyday
Lock and key in imagination be
Going out free and easily
But a fear of outside keeping
Person under cover inside all day

Nothing sometimes to do and make
Time which is passing a lot
Knowing not what to do
In the minutes which pass by
Lost in the space never again to see

Emotional Ride

An emotional ride it is
That an individual could be on
Sitting although not physically but
In a psychologically locked state

Open for a mix of emotions
Anger for a loneliness inside
Anxiety of what could be next
Grief for the time passed which is a waste
Knowing not the things to do
In the minutes which constantly and
continuously
Flow to be a series of wasted days next

River

Down from the distant place you come
Clear as a crystal glass to see and enjoy
A life giver are you to one and all
Coming regularly without missing

Animals and birds alike enjoy your calm
But when violent not a single one can stop
For in anger you will swallow whole
The earth as it is fully
Water you be there constantly
Forever for existence to continue safely

Hope

Hope is a word which brings
A day of light in a darkness
Leading to a way out into
The world full and filled with opportunities

A path that hope shows in time
Two way road leading the person
To a good and bad path showing and giving
But the choice which is to be done
In the life and hand of the individual
Whose decision in the end will have
Happy or a sad result depending
On the answer chosen whatever it be

Chances

A life in full is what is had
In this birth which has to be spent
Leading a happy day was I
One after the other for a year and the next

Coming to an end has it now, for
To start a new chapter in life
Is but a unique opportunity given
One chance only there
To have a goodness at present

Tree Goddess

Looking at her who is a beauty
No matter from which side you look
To touch at the root of all are you
A hard and strong firmness to feel

Growing up a sense of happiness you have
A smile on a person's face whenever in sight
You are brown at the bottom but green above
Surrounding everywhere, with a small seed you
sprout
To grow slowly but steadily, a necessity you are
For the existence of life all around

Blast of Happiness

Light, a small day of sunshine
In a hollow cave of darkness
Given to think a positive thought
Not a negative one as before

Thinking only along a positive line
Gives a blast of happiness
Never seen before not will be seen
In the days which will come
For that blast is here only to stay

Opportunity

An opportunity when given should
Be used by the one for whom
It be given as when there be hope
Should try out the possibility
For another time know not the individual
When once again if next a try be given

Using and working on all the chances
To make life better than yesterday
A future where to bring a start
On a new chapter which is to pass

Procrastination

Do today what can be done tomorrow
In the future you think of things to do
Making a list or a schedule to complete
But know not if a time might come
When to finish the work you will be

Passing on to the next day
What you have time to do on this day
Procrastination is an ill habit built
Overcome it and do today all the work

For you never know what the future
Might bring to pass, for tomorrow
Is a new day which is there
A new chapter in life which is yet not come to
pass

Freedom

Freedom is something which is
A wish held by everyone
Through life which is full of ties

Going forward the individual has
Decisions to make and choices from
Which one has to be chosen so as to
Make the way ahead a clear and
A neat road in which to live

Choices

Choices are something which
Everyone is given in life
The freedom to choose the right
Is something which at times is difficult
If the individual then knows not
Difference between the right and wrong

A right in one's life can be a wrong
In the life of another who is there
So choices are there for us to decide
Wisely and carefully for sometimes
You have one chance only

Wakeup Call

A wake- up call needed by you
Who sleeping know not the outside
Which changing constantly and continuously
With the flow of time non-stop

Pat given on the back work not
A blaring alarm and a knock in the head
To bring a change in the self
So as to raise out there
In the reality seen everywhere

Gratitude

"Gratitude" a word so short and sweet
But such a powerful meaning it has
Shown to any individual practically
Be it with only a small loving smile to be seen

Making the other's heart swell with
A happiness and joy which in turn
Will again be shown with a huge helping nature
Learnt maybe in a basic theory lesson
But seen in practice with eyes wide to see

Blessings

A miracle truly in the life
Of every person rich or poor
An example, the growth and birth
Of a small baby from the womb
To show and stay in the wide world there be

Blessing from an elder given positively
We all sees miracle in change brought
Be it in the life physically or mentally
Seen in the happiness and a smile which is
An inner feeling can't be bought simply
No matter how wealthy a person there be

Happiness

Working hard for a way to live
No matter the stress and tension which may be
To live a wealthy life which may be sorrow
filled
Thinking now I am wealthy happiness is a given
Not dare a thought to the sickness ahead

People live their whole lives not knowing
Happiness is not outside, for it be
A source of emotion and feeling inside
Brought out by a choice
From the side of the individual whoever it is

For happiness doesn't lie outside in the wide
world
It is an elixir which lies within
Choose happiness in whatever you see and are
Then only is life worth living for

Goals

Goals can be made by the mind
Whenever the desire be thought of
To bring stars and a creamy glow
On the face of the individual who think of it

But just a theory can never be of use
If in practice it is not put out to see
For the results whatever it may be
Lead on with just a little hardwork and
determination
To gain all achievements you are worthy to
attain

The Mind

Strength of mind is a gift
To think positive no matter what there be
The situation which the person be involved in
Power given to solve anything at the snap of the
finger
Whatever the circumstances in front

Negativity shown is poisonous, may it be
In the thought of action of an individual
Leading to harm for not the other but oneself
So think positive and act good no matter
What the time and circumstance it maybe
To grow up to as great a height as there is

Energy

Excitement is a wish to do things
With energy that brims and bursts from within
To do the work that is set forth with a wish
Of perfection that automatically comes

Working with enthusiasm and energy will
Set the individual 's life straight
For life be great if the person works with skill
No matter the barriers which come ahead

You will break through every barrier for an
achievement
Got from hardwork done with strength
Mentally and physically brought out by
The energy which in reality the individual
already has

Adequacy

Sleep is a boon for the body of an individual
Done adequately , the necessity is a must
But as everyone says in the quote or saying
'Too much is too bad ' is something
Which applies here too, for you and the rest

Like food when eaten adequately gives energy
To conquer the whole wide world seen
But overeating brings obesity and a laziness
Under eating , a malnourishment and weakness

This applies to life also for life is
A great balancing act for everyone
So do everything with skill and correctly
Will you succeed is a question asked
Which will turn out 100% true
For the person in question will achieve
Everything the individual will put hands to do

Doubts

Doubtful yet never giving in
To the fixation which the mind lives in
Everyday not a new but the same
Existing thoughts continue to haunt
Bringing a torment to both body and mind

Knowing the correct solution for
Yet searching near and everywhere
Seeking for a way to solve a problem
That is already with thy itself

Look not on the outside for everything
For you will never find a single thing
Present and future are in hand
A choice there is only once to choose
It is up to you whether you choose right or
wrong

Abilities

'Strength lies in numbers' is but
A quote to say on certain occasions
Like a war which is to be fought
When winning at times may be uncertain

For strength in numbers can also fail when
It comes to lack of capability of an individual
Ability is shown in the skill a person has
A single individual can bring a shocking change
One person is strong enough to bring
Changes larger which thousands can't

Capacity is shown on how a person uses
Qualities and abilities given to him or her
How the capabilities given is used is
But another question to be asked
Positively or negatively is a choice left
To the individual in whom capacity is given

Grudge

A grudge held by a person is
But a weakness which in the long run
Can prove to be fatal for the individual
themselves
For anger is an emotion which can put
Distance between friends and people uselessly

Bringing a smile on one's face increases
Happiness of the person and those around
Follow the saying 'Laughter is the best medicine
'

Think happy thoughts and choose
A stress free and joyful long life

Role Play

The role of a brother or sister be it younger or
older
Can never be filled by a friend in need
For only a single child knows the pain felt
Of being the only child of parents at home

Learning from the elders and teaching the
younger
Is a joy which is beyond compare which
The parents and grandparents can never fulfilled
No matter the time be it finite or infinite

To go on the joy of life ahead
Lessons learnt from a sibling is always
In the mind of every individual be it young or
old
For its necessity there is to people
To be and do good wherever they go

Mother

A mother's place can never be filled
By another no matter the time or place
Time moves on never stopping for anyone
But a mother is there for everyone

To lay our head on her lap when
Sadness engulfs the mind to cry ourhearts out
Or but and miss the mother tightly and joyfully
During the times of happiness

Eating the food prepared by her
Is beyond compare for there is no other
In the eyes of the child who can prepare
And imitate the tasty food prepared

When in need the mother is there
Although others leave scared of loss to
themselves
But mom is always there to first fulfill
The child's needs before her own come forth

Comforts

Leaning against a soft pillow gives
A great comfort which in words can be
Given a description by the one who experienced
As it is a joy beyond compare

But at the same time leaning against
A rock, hard and rough causes a discomfort
Whose effect is told in immediate words
No matter what and how the outcome might be

Positive and negative is something from which
A lot can be learnt of individual needs
So choose wisely what you want to lean on
Comfort of familiarity or discomfort of hard
work
Is an answer given by the participant whose
hands it be

Service

Thinking always of thyself will bring
No big thing expect sorrow of mind
Happiness there lies in service to
Whoever is in need, whatever
Might be the the time of the day

Goal achievement done for selfish needs
Will always being a consequence
At present no-one knows when it might happen
But remember always service to others
To find solutions to the problems they face

Will bring a light of hope no matter how dark
The circumstances of the individual who brings
Service to others first always and second
Only attention comes to their own needs
However difficult the situation may be

Desires

Desire is something which is bad
By each and every individual
Whoever is in earth alive there be
But a very thin line there is always
Between for what the person's desires will be

A good thing to desire and fulfill will
Bring happiness in the hearts of
Everyone who is involved in the situation

Bad thoughts and desires serve only
To bring darkness which in turn
Will switch off and suck out all the light
There is in the life of the individual
No matter the time or date it be

Innocence

Innocence a quality so life
Found in all from birth
But circumstances change and perspectives
change
As an infant does become an adult with the
passage of time

Always know light and dark do-exist
For one can't be alive without the other inside
For choices you make are yours alone
For that is the unique opportunity given to man

Choosing to do the good or bad things
Is what the answer to all the questions in life
So choose how for there is no time to waste
As time may be infinite but mortal life is finite

Purity

The purity of thought brought by
An overload of innocence in each minute
That passes swiftly as time flows on
In the stark reality of the real world

Innocence a quality found but, in a handfu,l
Be it breathing humans or other animals
Time moves on to bring a dark glow over
The white beauty of innocence which is present

But worry not oh people for there is
An opportunity within is unique to each person
To choose the goodness of light or the
Badness of the darkness in the life ahead

Clarity

Modesty and pride traits so very contrasting
Constantly are they fighting for dominance
Which will win is a constant question
unanswered
By the individual undergoing such startling
experiences

The sweetness and softness brought by modesty
Is that which brings happiness in those all
around
The arrogance and ignorance brought by pride
Is nothing but that which tears a person apart

Knowing everything about a subject is
But an impossibility, as thoughts determine
The knowledge a person has is finite or infinite
Based on the thoughts which the individual
chooses to have
For yearning to learn good or bad things in this
life

For choice is a unique quality given to man
Choosing to do good or bad in this life they live
As time may be infinite but the portion given
To every individual in this world is but finite

Beauty and the Beast

Fear that something might happen
Will not let you see the beauty
Just like the curtains which close the window
Prevent us from seeing the bright blue sky
Being scared lets you see not what is outside

Hiding behind the curtain protects you not
As time will move ahead outside
And day will be over and night will come just as
it does everyday
So remove your fear and come outside
To see and hear the beauty of the world with
Eyes and ears brimming with joy

Rage

Ignited like a dark red blaze
Rage from within raises out
To consume that which is all around in its path

Humans can either chanalize this blaze
Into the good and positive things they do
Or burn down themselves with the negatives
This is the choice an individual will have to
make
When the fire of rage blazes uncontrolled within